THE MAGIC TRACTOR

A Pantomime
by
PAT BOND

Published by:
New Playwrights' Network
35 Sandringham Road
Macclesfield
Cheshire
SK10 1QB

ISBN 0 86319 117 7

STAGE PLANS

Act I. Sc. i. Widow Jackpenny's Farm.

Backcloth. Clearly defined fields, very blue sky. woolly clouds. trees. Bright and bold.

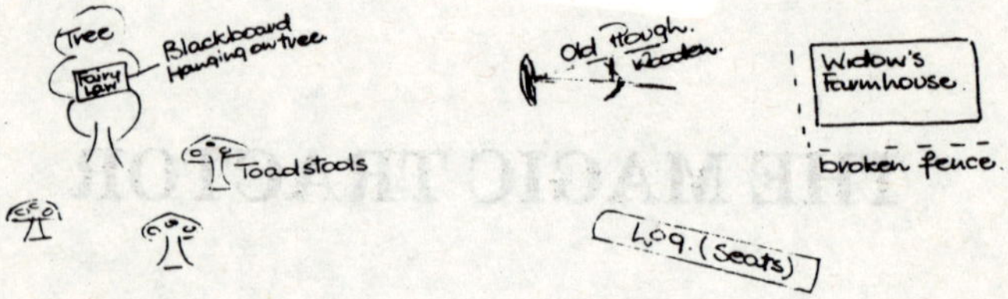

Act I. Sc ii At Baron Grabalotts.

Backcloth as Sc i.

Act I Sc iii

Backcloth as Sc. i

Set as Sc. i with addition of ladder, boxes bucket.

Stage Plans.

Act II Sc I. The Wild Wood.

Backcloth of sinister looking trees with evil faces and claw like branches.

No scenery - for the trees (girls) see production notes.

Act II Sc. II The Professor's Factory.

Backcloth of complicated piping, machinery using beer cans (Emmett style.)

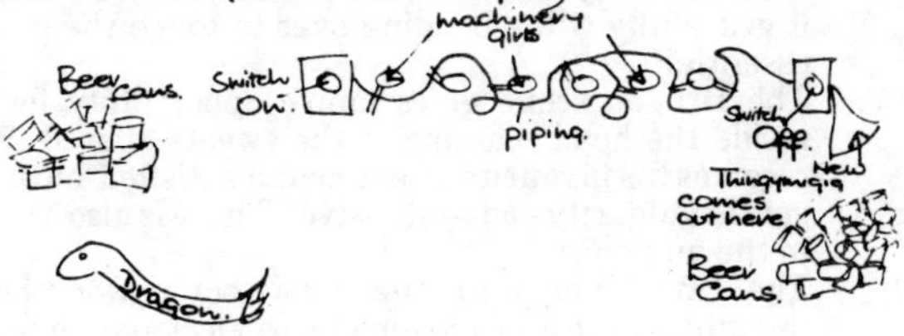

Act II Sc. III The Fairies Graduation.

This can be played in front of tabs for ease of changing set behind.

Act II Sc IV All Ends Well.

Backcloth as Opening. Farmhouse smartened up, fence mended, perhaps a window box or some other sign of change in fortune.

PRODUCTION NOTES

Although not one of the well-known pantomime stories "The Magic Tractor" has all the ingredients of this type of entertainment - fairies, good and bad; Dame; Principal Boy etc. With a very obvious rural flavour it is particularly suitable for a village production, especially in a farming area, and was first produced by Wymondham Young Farmers Club in Norfolk in January 1983.

There are many opportunities to introduce local references and jokes. The songs, of course, are recommended only, and subject to the usual permission to perform from the Performing Rights Society, but "Farmer On A Bike" is a must!

The Wild Wood scene, with soft music playing, is meant to be beautiful - take care it does *not* become funny - and lighting is important here. The 'trees' are actresses in green net costumes and twiggy head-dresses. Their fingers are extended, clawlike, with twigs to pluck at Tom and Lucy. When the Good Fairy touches each tree with her wand it gracefully wilts, bending over to touch the ground (good backs are essential!).

The Dragon scene gives ample opportunity for fun, with the actor inside the head reacting to the sweets offered. When, eventually, he receives his favourite sweetmeat a satisfied 'burp' can be heard (a little gentle vulgarity - non-offensive). There is also a chance to throw sweets to the audience.

The 'machinery' in the Professor's workshop gives scope for imaginative use of movement to electronic music - a row of girls in black trousers and sweaters with silver gloves and helmets and linked by flexible piping wound round them is very effective - it needs careful rehearsal to ensure the actions are synchronized. When the Professor switches on and off they must start and stop together.

The use of the auditorium for entrances is recommended and the banishment of Nightshade to the back of the hall is especially effective. Help in quickly changing her appearance to her new image is needed and the audience should, of course, be unaware of what is happening behind them.

Big, bold backcloths of the children's story book type fit this production best.

WIDOW LACKPENNY	Traditional Dame. Poorly dressed (panto medieval) with darns and patches etc. until her fortune changes, then richly costumed and bewigged.
LUCY	Pretty principal Girl, well dressed as befits a Baron's daughter. Determined to fight for her Tom though not wishing to hurt her father.
TOM	Principal Boy. Shabbily dressed until Finalé. Needs support of Lucy, to whom he has lost his heart, to spur him on.
BARON GRABALOTT	Wicked Baron, greedy for the Widow's land. Changes character towards end (? for his own ends). Possessive towards Lucy whom he loves. Well dressed - purple good colour - boots, cloak, high brimmed hat & riding crop.
BILL	Important comic characters best spoken in broad dialect
BEN	Simple country yokels far from happy with their lot. Wear simple straight jerkins with names on back - identical costumes.
TEACHER FAIRY	The "School Marm" fairy, with tinsel trimmed mortar board and gown. Definitely in charge but retaining 'fairy' qualities.
FAIRY GARDENIA	The Good Fairy - white costume with touches of pink. Appropriate flower head-dress and wand.
FAIRY NIGHTSHADE	The Bad Fairy - sludgy green costume, appropriate head-dress and wand. Face and eyes carefully made-up with green tinge or mask over eyes, making it easier to transform to more attractive fairy when required.
PIXIE GARY	'Fun' part which must be played straight. The urge to play in 'camp' style should be resisted. Bright green traditional elfin costume with pointed shoes and cap. Gold pointed collar and cap for Finalé. Must talk to audience with confidence.

Cont'd

FAIRY ROSE
FAIRY BLUEBELL
FAIRY POPPY — All Fairies dressed in colours to match their names.

FAIRY GODETIA
FAIRY LOBELIA
FAIRY BUTTERCUP

PROFESSOR — Vague, bustling character more "Doctor Who" than "Wizard" in dress.

OLD WOMAN — The Good Fairy in disguise, best played by another actress for ease of costuming. Shawl, long skirt etc.

URNITRUDE — Small but important part - Tinny's true love. Dressed after the style of a milk churn with only the face showing, but with definite feminine touches - bows, frills etc. Tinny kind of voice is best.

DRAGON — Enjoys sweets, but only his favourites. Roaring and tail-swishing amuse (and frighten) children. Munching noises made on discovery of right sweets.

TINNY TRACTOR — Important to maintain magical property - the driver should not be visible from any angle. Made after the style of Ivor the Engine, complete with face and mouth controlled from inside to turn up or down. Voice needs a tinny quality - a radio microphone inside is a help. Don't spoil the illusion by allowing the driver to appear in the Finalé. Could have own music or signature tune.

ASSEMBLY LINE, TREES, FASHION MODELS

ACT I
Scene 1 - Widow Lackpenny's Farm
Scene 2 - At Baron Grabalott's
Scene 3 - In The Farm Yard

ACT II
Scene 1 - The Wild Wood
Scene 2 - The Professor's Factory
Scene 3 - The Fairies' Graduation
Scene 4 - All Ends Well

ACT I

Scene 1
Widow Lackpenny's Farm

MUSIC —'Opening Chorus Of Fairies from "Iolanthe".'
The scene opens with FAIRIES at play near the widow's farm. Two or three are throwing a flower ball to one another. One is skipping with a flower rope, which is turned by two others.
FAIRY POPPY is combing her hair and looking in a mirror. FAIRY DEADLY NIGHTSHADE stands apart from the others, sulkily tapping her foot..
There is a blackboard hanging on a tree, with toadstool seats scattered around it. On the other side of the stage Widow Lackpenny's tumbledown farmhouse can be seen.
TEACHER FAIRY enters and, clapping her hands, calls the FAIRIES around her. She carries a silver-trimmed pointer and a book clearly labelled 'FAIRY LAW'; she points to the same words written at the top of the blackboard.

TEACHER: Come Fairies, gather round me please
Fairy Bluebell, do not tease
I'll test you now, one at a time
And don't forget, your words must rhyme
For that's the way all Fairies talk
Oh, dearie me, where *is* my chalk?

ROSE: *(Pointing to NIGHTSHADE)*
I know, I know just who has got it

Hidden in her dark green pocket

TEACHER: Well now I need it in my hand
To write so you will understand
So bring it here, you naughty sprite
For on this board I'm going to write
Because before you leave this school
You must know each fairy rule.

(FAIRIES react with consternation — NIGHTSHADE gives chalk reluctantly)

BLUEBELL: Oh dear, oh dear, I'm not too clever
Pass this test — don't think I'll ever!

POPPY: I wish I'd studied at my books
Instead of caring for my looks

TEACHER: Now what comes first in fairy law?

GODETIA: Be always kind and help the poor

TEACHER: That's very good, what have we next?

GARDENIA: Stay always sweet however vexed

TEACHER: I see that you've been learning well

LOBELIA: Please teacher, what about a spell?

TEACHER: Ah yes, a spell but have a care
There's very few of them to spare
Our bank of spells, hit by inflation
We're quite a hard-up fairy nation

BUTTERCUP: But surely we can each have one
If not, we shan't have any fun

TEACHER: I know my dear, it shall be so
But there's more to learn before you go

(FAIRY NIGHTSHADE has taken no part in the lesson)

NIGHTSHADE: I'm sick of learning this and that
And don't eat this or you'll be fat
Nectar must be cholesterol free
Go tell that to the honey bee
Whoever heard of a tubby fairy?
Like thistledown we're light and airy.

(Floats around stage)

I know you've said that to be wise
It's early bed and early rise
But not till the dandelion head
Tells me it's late will I go to bed.
And as for rising bright and early
You can't expect that of me, surely?

I cannot wait to get away
Enjoy myself, have fun and play
I know it all so you've no need
To lecture me and make me heed.

TEACHER: Oh Nightshade dear, it is a shame
That you have such a deadly name
If you'd been christened pink geranium
There'd be kinder thoughts within your cranium
But there it is, I fear that you
Behaving as you always do
Will not heed me but go your way
Whatever I advise or say
Now fairies come, it's time for me
To say goodbye and set you free
You have one month till you return
To try your F.C.S. to earn.

(FAIRY BLUEBELL comes to front of stage and tells audience F.C.S. stands for Fairies Certificate of Spells)

TEACHER: Fairies, now before you go
A little song — soh-la-de-doh

(FAIRIES arrange themselves as a choir — NIGHTSHADE apart — TEACHER conducts Opening Chorus of Fairies from 'Iolanthe' — 'We are dainty little fairies etc.'

(Form into circle, link hands and dance)

'We must dance and we must sing
Round about our fairy ring.'

(Break to say good-bye. Music continues as FAIRIES trip off, shaking hands and curtsying to TEACHER. NIGHTSHADE comes forward to shake hands, very reluctantly)

TEACHER: Oh, Nightshade, you will have no friends
If you pursue your wicked ends
So go now, change your ways, be kind
And maybe if you do, you'll find
That you'll be loved where'er you go
I promise you it could be so.

NIGHTSHADE: *(Moving Downstage; to audience)*
Isn't she stupid, don't you agree?
But I don't care, I'm free, I'm free!

[EXIT

TEACHER: And now all signs of us must go
So there is nothing left to show
That we were here — come, Pixie Gary.

(Claps hands and raises voice. To Audience)

(He's the one to fetch and carry)
All dressed in his suit of elfin green
The smartest gnome you've ever seen.

(Enter PIXIE GARY in bright elfin green suit)

PIXIE GARY: Here I am, Teacher — now what's next?
At times she makes me very vexed.

(To Audience)

She's very bossy, can't you see
How she always picks on me?
I'll join the Pixie Union and they'll make me a brother
Then have a care, you Teacher, or there'll be a spot of bother.

(TEACHER has been generally tidying up during this speech)

TEACHER: Now come along and do your work
I cannot bear an elf to shirk
Just move these stools from here to there.
Gently now — oh, have a care
Mortals don't know just where we play
Do hurry up — don't take all day.

[Exit

(PIXIE comes to Front of Stage)

PIXIE GARY: It's Gary this and Gary that
I'm used just like an old doormat
No time for me to woo my Rose
I'd hoped one day I could propose
Then be a Dad, that should show you
That I am not a fairy too!

[Exit with scissor jump

(Enter WIDOW who begins her speech turned away from the audience)

WIDOW: Oh dear, oh dear, how my feet hurt. Think I'll just have a little rest and take off my boots. That's funny, *(Local shop)* must have sold me odd socks again— that's the second time they've done that, I've another pair just like these in the pantry (well I like to be tidy) I shall complain that's what I'll do — yes, I shall complain — I'll wait until the shop is full of people then I'll say — now see here Mr... *(Turns and sees audience)* Oh, hullo — I didn't see you there..how are you, all right? It's these socks you see, I do try to be smart. I suppose your socks are both the same colour, you never know, perhaps you'd better look. Come along now, up with those trouser legs, don't be shy...no Madam, not you! I could do with a new pair of shoes — aren't they expensive?...I wonder? If you plant an apple

tree, you get? *(To audience)* If you plant a pear tree, you get? If you plant a shoe tree? I'll tell you why I'm so poor — I own a small farm, you know what a farm is, don't you? A few acres covered by mortgage. Since I've been a poor widow woman things have gone from bad to worse.
(Enter TOM)

WIDOW: This is my son Tom, a dear boy, he has his father's eyes, my nose...

TOM: And cousin Willie's trousers! *(Shows trousers with patch)*

WIDOW: What are we going to do Tom? That Baron Grabalott next door is determined to take our land.

TOM: Don't worry Ma, something will turn up, he wouldn't turn us out — our family has been here for years and years.

WIDOW: Yes son, when your Grandpappy came here all the Archer's had was an allotment!

TOM: That must have been a long time ago. Why did you marry father, Ma?

WIDOW: He told me he was in something big with cattle in *(Name of County)*

TOM: Wasn't he?

WIDOW: Oh yes, he drove the meat van for *(Local Shop)* the butchers.

TOM: Were you always poor?

WIDOW: Poor? We were so poor your father couldn't afford shoes — he used to paint his feet brown and lace up his toes. You had a rough time too — when you were a baby, I couldn't afford to buy talcum powder to put on your...

TOM: Mother!! That was a long time ago...what are we going to do now? If the fields are not tended we shall surely be turned out. There's no money for wages, Dobbin is getting too feeble to work. What we need is a tractor, not these old wooden ploughs. *(Points to old wooden plough. Both sit — head in hands — half turned away from audience, almost asleep. No reaction as FAIRY GARDENIA enters right)*

GARDENIA:
What have we here, they look so sad
This poor old dame and handsome lad
I wonder if perhaps I might
Help them in their sorry plight
Now if a tractor's what they want
To help them plough and rake and plant
A magic one I could provide
That will not need a man inside

So as it works upon the soil
Tom can rest from endless toil.

(Enter FAIRY NIGHTSHADE from left)

NIGHTSHADE: *(To FAIRY GARDENIA)*
You think you're clever and you'll pass
Out at the top of the fairy class
Because you're always sweet and kind
But it's not so easy this you'll find
With me to spoil your magic trick
You are so good, you make me sick.

GARDENIA: Oh Deadly, won't you be my friend
And let this silly quarrel end?

NIGHTSHADE: Be friends with you, that I'll never
You'll find out I'm far too clever.

[Exit

GARDENIA: *(Front of stage to audience)*
Will you instead be friends with me?
Just raise your hands and let me see
I'm happier now I know you're there
Please shout if Nightshade should appear
Now I must go and work my spell
But first these two I'd better tell.

(Casts spell. Flash appears from side of stage. GARDENIA whispers to TOM and WIDOW with hand round mouth — shows audience she has told them and stands back to watch. WIDOW, slowly waking up, looks pleased though wondering)

WIDOW: Tom, I must have dozed off, and had such a strange dream — oh it was lovely — I dreamt there was a brand new tractor in the barn.

TOM: That's funny Ma. I had the same dream.

WIDOW: Tom, you don't think...

(TOM and WIDOW look at each other both having the same thought)

TOM: Oh Mother — let's go and look.

(TOM and WIDOW exit)

GARDENIA: I've cast the spell now wait and see
Things will improve with help from me.

NIGHTSHADE: You think that this will end your trouble
I'm off to spoil that, at the double.

[Exit

GARDENIA: I see that I shall have to stay
Till Deadly Nightshade goes away

Don't forget to give a shout
Whenever you see her about
Listen, I think it's coming now
Tinny the Tractor, take a bow.

(Noise of TRACTOR heard off stage. Enter TRACTOR — stop in centre of stage — TOM and MOTHER walking behind very pleased. Music very tinny)

TINNY TRACTOR: I'm Tinny the Tractor that's who I am
I don't run on diesel or eat bread and jam
There's not many like me, I'm a magic machine
The furrows I plough are all straight and clean
I don't work by day but only at night
For without a driver I'd give you a fright
But I know what to do, like the good fairy said
To help Widow Lackpenny out of the red.

CURTAIN

END OF SCENE 1

SCENE 2

In front of curtains. Heard offstage — BILL 'No' BEN 'Yes you will'. Enter BILL and BEN from right

BILL: I'm not telling him — you'll have to.

BEN: Don't be such a Silly Billy — of course you'll tell him.

BILL: But I'm scared...he'll be f-f-furious.

BEN: We must tell him when he's in a good mood.

BILL: When's that?

BEN: He can be all right — sometimes.

BILL: Never! He was educated at the John McEnroe Charm School. Why he's got the sort of face that always wants to see the manager.

BEN: Well what are we going to do — he said if that field was not ploughed, then she was to be turned out.

BILL: And now it has been ploughed — how? That old horse of theirs couldn't have pulled a plough.

BEN: I don't know how it's been done but it has and you've got to tell him.

BILL: Oh no, I haven't.

BEN: Oh yes, you have.

(Involving audience)

BILL: Oh no I haven't.

BEN: Oh yes you have etc.etc.

BILL: Well whoever tells him had better have his running boots on.

BEN: Don't worry — we'll tell him together — after all we're friends we must stick together.

SONG — Friendship

BEN: Now let's go and get it over.
(Exit right. Curtains open. LUCY is on stage alone. Enter BARON from right)

BARON: *(Loudly, very cross)* Where are they — why aren't they here?

LUCY: Father dear, please don't get so cross.

BARON: *(Big change of voice)* Cross, me cross? *(Tells audience ingratiatingly)* Why I'm the gentlest, sweetest man in all the world. Cross — ha,ha, cross — me? Bill, Ben.
(BILL and BEN enter, each trying to hide behind the other)

BILL and BEN: Yes, sire, did you call? Here we are, sire, did you want us? *(Etc. etc. Confusion)*

BARON: You idle good-for-nothings. Don't know why I pay you.

BEN: *(Aside)* You don't.

BARON: What was that? Now — have you served the papers on Widow Lackpenny?

BILL: N...n...no Sir.

BARON: No...*No*...NO? And why haven't you, if I might ask?

BEN: Because...

BILL: Because...

BILL and BEN: Because the field has been ploughed and...

BARON: What?

BEN: Yes sire, the field has...

BARON: Ploughed, *ploughed, PLOUGHED?* How has it been ploughed? *(Voice rises)*

BILL: We don't know, sire. Last night when we looked it hadn't been done but now it's...ploughed.

BARON: How can I say the widow is neglecting the land if the ploughing is done? You must find out who is helping her.

BEN: Perhaps *(Fill in appropriate name from audience)* lent her a tractor.

BARON: He wouldn't lend anyone a tractor — he's too mean. He might do it for a price but where would she get the money? You must find out — creep round and see what you can find out.

BILL: I'd rather...not. *(Very nervously, visibly trembling)*

BEN: Shush. *(To BILL)* The widow has a son you know, sire.

LUCY: *(To herself)* And what a son!

BARON: What did you say, daughter.

LUCY: Oh, nothing, father.

BARON: That son couldn't have helped — he's another good for nothing.

LUCY: *(Going to father)* Oh no, father, he isn't, he isn't. *(Protesting)*

BARON: Isn't he, my girl? And what do you know about him?

LUCY: I've only...seen him father.

BARON: Just you make sure I don't catch you talking to him — I'm very particular about *my* daughter's friends.

LUCY: That's why I haven't got any.

BARON: *(To BILL and BEN)* Now be off with you and see what you can find out and *do something* I want that land.

[BILL and BEN exit left

I want that land and I intend to get it hook or by crook. I want to be the biggest landowner in the land, I want to rule the county, the country perhaps even the world. I want to be Chairman of *(Appropriate name)* Town Council and I will — then things will be different, you'll see.

SONG - If I Ruled The World.

LUCY: Oh father, I liked it better before you were so ambitious — you were happy then.

BARON: Nonsense child, we're happy now.

[Exit right

LUCY: Happy? I'm not happy — I'm miserable. What use are money and fine clothes if you're unhappy. Father wasn't like this when poor Mama was alive.
(Enter TOM stealthily from left)

TOM: Has he gone?

LUCY: Who?

TOM: Your father of course. It wouldn't do for him to see us together.

LUCY: He would certainly be very cross, he doesn't like me to have any friends. He says he wants to keep me all to himself.

TOM: I'd like to keep you all to myself too.

LUCY: *(Sits)* Dear Tom — sit and talk to me for a little while, cheer me up for I'm very miserable.

TOM: *(Sits)* What shall we talk about? It's been cold lately, hasn't it?

LUCY: Yes.

TOM: Did you know that it's so cold at the North Pole that the inhabitants live somewhere else?

LUCY: Tom!

TOM: I went to the doctor last week because my tongue looked furry — he said it had grown a fur coat to keep warm because I'd eaten so much frozen food.

LUCY: *(Laughing)* You are funny, Tom. I feel better already.

TOM: *(Rising)* But I have something to tell you which will really make you happy — we have a tractor to help with the work.

LUCY: *(Up to TOM)* A tractor, Tom? Where did you get it?

TOM: That's the strange part, Lucy. It just came and it's magic — it knows what to do and... *(Looking round to make sure no-one is listening)* ...it talks.

LUCY: It talks?!

TOM: Yes, I've heard it when it thinks there's nobody about...and it can sing!

LUCY: But, Tom, what does it sing?

TOM: Oh, it goes something like this —

We three upon the farm,
Working night and day you'll see
Tinny Tractor, the Widow and T.

(Tune from 'Lovejoy, Enoch and Me' — Happidrome Radio programme)

LUCY: What a funny little song, Tom — but who's 'T'?

TOM: Why, me of course, Lucy. T for Tom, only Tom wouldn't rhyme.

LUCY: How silly of me! What a dear little song, I like it and I'm sure I shall like your magic tractor. *(To AUDIENCE)* You will as well, won't you, children? *(Reaction. To TOM)* You must have a good fairy looking after you, Tom. Perhaps if the farm makes money father might let us marry after all.

TOM: So you see, it's not been such a bad day, after all.

LUCY: And we've had a really happy talk. Sometimes, Tom, when I'm all alone and feeling miserable, I pretend that you and I can be alone somewhere — just the two of us with no-one to say we mustn't be friends.

TOM: Where's that, Lucy?

LUCY: On an island where the sun is always shining, imagine it, Tom... *(Looking mistily into the distance)* ...just you and me...

TOM: That's a lovely dream, Lucy — just you and me — talking and dreaming together.

(LUCY and TOM sing 'Happy Talk' from 'South Pacific' from the side of the stage.
After they have sung the song once through, half curtains open to reveal GIRLS behind gauze creating a dream scene in which they mime to the words of the song. It is suggested that half are dressed as

boys, with ragged trousers and straw hats — the other half in South Sea Islanders costume. LUCY and TOM are unaware of the sequence. Just as the song ends the BARON is heard offstage shouting BILL and BEN. Half curtains close)

TOM: Here comes your father — he mustn't find me here.

LUCY: Goodbye, Tom. Come and find me again soon, it's been lovely to share my dream with you.

[TOM exits

BARON: *(Striding on from Right, rather cross)* Where are they?

LUCY: Who, father?

[Exit

BARON: Why, those scallywags, of course — those good-for-nothing rascals.

BILL and BEN: *(Entering Left)* Did you call, Master?

BARON: Of course I called! Where have you been?

BEN: Where you told us, Master.

BILL: We looked in the Widow's barn.

BARON: And...?

BEN: We found a...

BILL: We found a...

BARON: Speak up! What did you find?

BILL and BEN: We found a...tractor.

BARON: *A tractor?*

BEN: Yes, and it's not like any tractor we've ever seen before.

BARON: What do you mean?

BEN: Well, it sort of... *(Lots of arm waving, showing size and shape)*

BILL: And it's got a... *(Demonstrating)*

BEN: But not like this...

BILL: No, more like that.

BARON: Stop, stop. Never mind what it looks like — where did she get it? She hasn't any money, couldn't pay me the rent last month — surely she hasn't got a bank manager in her cupboard?

BILL: No — there wasn't one in there last time she opened it — it was quite bare.

BEN: Like Mother Hubbard!

(Snatch of song 'Old Mother Hubbard' and a little dance from BILL and BEN)

BARON: *(Intervening)* Stop this at once! I don't pay you to sing silly songs.

BEN: *(To AUDIENCE)* He doesn't pay us to do anything!

BILL: He *doesn't pay!*

BARON: I must do something at once.

BILL and BEN: *(To AUDIENCE)* He means *we* must do something at once!

BARON: *You* must stop it working.

BILL and BEN: *(To AUDIENCE)* We told you so.

BEN: What shall we do?

BARON: I don't know, twist something, push something, pull something, take something away — I don't know, but *do something!* If you don't stop that tractor working, it will be the worse for you. Ah-ha

[Exit right

BILL: What are we going to do, Ben?

BEN: Perhaps we can twist the thingamy.

BILL: Or change the whatsit.

BEN: Make a hole in the hooj-a-ma-flip etc.etc.

BILL: Oh Ben, I wish we didn't have to do the Baron's dirty work for him. He's got a lot of land already, he's rich like all farmers. Ben, I've never seen a farmer on a bike, have you?

SONG Farmer On A Bike — written by John Crisp. Ampersand Music, 33 Old Market Street, Thetford, Norfolk IP24 2EQ.

Old Farmer Palmer was on the other day
'Bout the price of his sugar beet drill,
He reckoned he'd found the little green pound
Don't pay them big red bills
Although he's got a private yacht
A racehorse and three cars
He always says the farm don't pay
That's how them farmers are.

Chorus

But I've never seen a farmer on a bike
I've never seen a farmer on a bike,
Wherever I've bin, I never miss a thing
But I've never see a farmer on a bike
He do complain about the rain

The greenfly or the drought
He say black spot have ruined his crop
But I can't make this out
I seen him get on a jumbo jet
I seen him on a train
But that'll be the day I see him
Bikin' down the lane.

I worked for Palmer till I wore my fingers to the bone
But when I speak of another pound a week
You ought to hear him moan
Although his combine cost a bomb
I'm sure you will agree
He could dispose of his Volvos
And bike about like me.

(CHORUS BILL and BEN exit. CURTAIN)

END OF SCENE 2

SCENE 3

It is night — TRACTOR can be seen in shed. Lights go out in farmhouse one at a time (A La 'The Waltons' T.V.Series)

WIDOW: *(Off stage)*Goodnight, Tom boy.

TOM: Goodnight, Mother.
(Noise of loud snoring. Enter BILL and Ben from right creeping and looking over shoulders)

BEN: This way Bill, it's over here.

BILL: All right Ben, I'm coming. *(Trips over bucket)*

BEN: Do be quite, you'll wake them up.

BILL: I don't like it Ben, I'm scared.

BEN: Don't be such a baby — where's your moral fibre?

BILL: In the packet in the pantry, Ben, I have it every morning. It's good for you, it makes you...

BEN: *(Quickly)* Not that kind of fibre, silly — if you're frightened, say your prayers.

BILL: I do — every night.

BEN: You should say them in the morning too.

BILL: I ain't scared in the morning.

BEN: Oh, come on! You keep watch while I look in the engine.
(Walks round looking carefully)

BILL: What can you see, Ben?

BEN: Funny, it's not like any engine I've seen before and there's no place for the driver to sit.

BILL: How does it work, Ben?

BEN: I don't know, it's a puzzle and no mistake. Come over here and we'll have a think. *(Go to side of stage — 'thinking' attitudes)*

TINNY TRACTOR:
Silly pair, they cannot know
I'm magic, that's what makes me go
There's only one part which would stop
Me working and that's on the top.

NIGHTSHADE: *(Has been listening from side of stage. To Audience)*
Did you hear what Tinny had to say?

To stop him now I know the way
I'll make sure they find that part
Then Tinny Tractor you'll not start.

BEN: Have you thunk, Bill?

BILL: Yes, Ben.

BEN: Well, what have you thunken?

BILL: We'll have to steal a part, Ben.

BEN: You silly Billy, I know that — but which part?

BILL: I don't know, Ben.

BEN: We'd better look again, but don't make a noise this time.
(BILL trips over bucket. Light goes on in upstairs window)

WIDOW: *(Off stage)* Who's that, is anyone there?

BEN: Only us chickens *(Chicken noises and actions)*

WIDOW: That's all right then, goodnight chickens.

BILL: I used to keep chickens.

BEN: I didn't know that.

BILL: Yes, thought I'd sell the eggs and make some money.

BEN: And did you?

BILL: What?

BEN: Make any money.

BILL: No. Can't understand it. Every week I sent them to *(Local market or auction)* to sell in their sale on Thursdays but they were never sold.

BEN: I'm not surprised, their sale is on Fridays. Were they big eggs?

BILL: Sort of middlin'.

BEN: What kind of chickens were they?

BILL: Middlin' sort.

BEN: I can't talk to you, you're stupid.

BILL: I know, Ben — you see I had this empty headed friend and we were always exchanging ideas — he's a teacher at *(Local school or College)* now, and I'm stupid.

BEN: Never mind, Billy boy. I'll look after you. Now let's try and put this tractor out of action and please the boss — we might even get some wages.
(DEADLY NIGHTSHADE guides their efforts and encourages them to look on top — much searching with aid of ladder, boxes etc. — this should be a real comedy routine)

BILL: What's this Ben?

BEN: I don't know, I've never seen one like it before. Can you unscrew it?

BILL: It's very stiff. *(Much effort)*

BEN: Oh!

BILL: I think it's coming.

BEN: Try harder, Bill... *(To audience)* ...Come on, you must help — one, two, three.

BILL: Yes, yes, it's turning — ah, here it is.

BEN: Good work, Bill. You're not so stupid after all.

BILL: Let's go and tell the gaffer.

[Exit

TINNY TRACTOR: *(To audience)*
You didn't shout, didn't you see,
What they were planning to do to me?

(DEADLY NIGHTSHADE comes forward from side of stage where she's been watching)

NIGHTSHADE: Ah ha, Gardenia, now you'll see
That you're not cleverer than me
Everything you do I'll spoil
All your spells I'll surely foil.

[Exit

TINNY TRACTOR :*(Mouth now turned down)*
You see me standing here forlorn
A piece of my insides is gorn
It was an unkind separation
A very nasty operation.

(Half curtains over. Stage lights up showing morning)

WIDOW: *(To audience, very jolly)* Good morning, good morning, isn't it a splendiferous morn? The birds are singing... *(Listens)* ...the cows are mooing, the bull is doing... *(Pause)* ...what bulls like to do! The sheep are baaing — oh, everything is simply splendid and I'm going to be rich like all the other farmers — well, if not rich then comfortable — you know, so that when I go to a restaurant I don't have to read the menu from right to left. *(To audience)* ...Think about it...prices on right, understand? I knew it was the bright lot in tonight. Of course, I've never been lucky — do you know someone once gave me a lovely suit with two skirts — I tore the jacket! But this tractor will make all the difference. We don't know where it came from but it works a treat...do you think my good fairy brought it? Do you believe in fairies (No, not that kind missus) I'm going to buy some new clothes — I'm so tired of always wearing hand-me-downs — I've never had anything new *(Aaaaahh from audience)* You know what I'm called, don't you? Secondhand Rose)

SONG Secondhand Rose.

(After song, parade of girls wearing odd mixtures of clothes)

WIDOW: Now here we have *(name)*she gets her clothes from the jumble sales in *(Local village)* very high class, that's where the posh people live. They throw out what the people in *(Local village)* wear for best. Here is *(name)*her brother is a *(Local football club)* supporter as perhaps you've guessed. Next comes *(name)* dressed in strawberry pink but the dress is slightly sticky — it's the jam you know, she bought it at *(Local)* Woman's Institute on the trading stall. And lastly, we have...she shops at a smart little boutique called Oxfam *(To audience)* Oh you know it too, do you madam. Oh yes, very smart — do stand up and let everyone see. *(Planted stooge - male - comes to stage from audience)* So you see, we're all Secondhand Roses.

(SONG BY ALL — Girls off. Curtain up)

TOM: *(Enterimg from left in great agitation)* Mother, mother, a dreadful thing has happened — the magic tractor won't start — I've tried everything and nothing will work.

WIDOW: Oh dear, just when I thought our troubles were over — now the Baron will take our land — he's sure to say we're not looking after it properly. Whatever shall we do Tom? We shall perish on the parish.

TOM: We shall what?

WIDOW: We shall perish on the parish.

TOM: Perish on the parish?

WIDOW: Yes — PERISH ON THE PARISH.

(As the 'p's are pronounced, Tom wipes eyes and shakes 'moisture' from hands — real comedy routine possible here)

LUCY: *(Enters right)* Hullo, you two, I say, you do look miserable.

WIDOW: I thought I was going to work the farm and pay off the mortgage to your father but now the tractor is broken and your father will say we're not looking after the land properly — he may be your father, Lucy, but he's a hard man, a hard man. *(Much pathos with comedy. Exit left)*

LUCY: Your poor Mother — she is upset — how can we help?

GARDENIA: *(Standing unseen. To audience)*
Such long, long faces — what's amiss?
They look so sad I can't have this.

TOM: I don't know what to do Lucy — I've never seen a tractor like this before — I can't mend it. And I don't know where it came from either.

GARDENIA: *(To audience)*
The tractor's broken, Deadly's about,
I wish you'd given me a shout
I've no more spells, they're rationed now
How can I help them, how, how, how?

LUCY: If only father would be more understanding. Shall I talk to him Tom?

TOM: I don't think that would do any good, Lucy, and he might send you away if he knew we were friends.

GARDENIA: *(To audience)*
I've just remembered an old friend
He lives at Bramerton Woods End
He has a little workshop theer
And makes all kinds of things — and beer
Professor What, that is his name
For a pet he keeps a dragon tame
Now in his factory while he's thinking
About new beers you could be drinking
He plans what else he can produce
From old beer cans, now no more use
I'm sure that he could make the part
We need to make poor Tinny start
The way to them I will unfold
But first I'll make myself look old
For a fairy they might not believe
So Lucy and Tom I must deceive.

[Exit right

LUCY: Oh dear Tom, if you have to give up the farm you'll go away and I shall never see you again. *(Cries, TOM comforts her)*

OLD WOMAN comes in right unnoticed (this is supposed to be Gardenia but is easier played by a similar sized actress). NIGHTSHADE in left — stays in shadows)

OLD WOMAN: What's this, crying on such a lovely day. What's the trouble pretty one?

LUCY: You don't want to hear our troubles, Granny.

OLD WOMAN: But I do, perhaps I could help.

TOM: Unless you know an inventor who can make a part for a magic tractor, I'm afraid, old woman, you cannot help us.

OLD WOMAN: But I can help you, I know just the man you want — the Professor, he can make anything — he uses old beer cans — he collects them after Young Farmers' parties, so he has plenty.

LUCY: Tom, do you think he could help?

TOM: We could go to see him and ask him. Where can we find him, Granny?

OLD WOMAN: You go along the road over there — follow that way — it is long, but do not take the short cut through the wild wood — remember my words well — do *not* take the short cut through the wild wood. Take the long way and you will find the Professor at the end of the wood. You will find a dragon sleeping nearby — he is rather fierce but if you give him sweets, he will let you pass — he is very fond of sweets but I cannot remember which ones he likes best.

LUCY: Quickly, Tom, let us go at once, there is no time to waste. Let us find this Professor and then perhaps tomorrow will be better.
(LUCY sings song 'Tomorrow')
Thank you Granny — you have been very kind — we shall not forget you.

TOM: Thank you, old woman. Goodbye.

[They exit

OLD WOMAN: I hope they remember what I told them for if they don't...

[Exit

NIGHTSHADE: *(To audience)*
I heard what she had to say
But I shall lead them far astray
Into the wood, that's where they'll go
That will make their progress slow.

[Exit

CURTAIN

END OF SCENE 3

END OF ACT I

ACT II

SCENE 1

Curtains open to show 'Wild Wood' girls in flimsy green drapery to resemble trees, arms outstretched menacingly with twigs incorporated. From side of stage

LUCY: *(Enters left — points to wood)* Oh Tom, are you sure this is the way, there is the wood and the old woman said we must not go that way.

(NIGHTSHADE's voice is heard off stage — softly calling 'Tom')

TOM: I thought I was following the road but I seemed to hear this voice telling me to come this way.

NIGHTSHADE: *(To audience)*
I'm sure you guessed, the voice he heard
Was not the song of singing bird
But mine — I'll lead them far astray
To make them take the long hard way.

LUCY: *(Pulling Tom back)* Oh Tom, I'm frightened — I'm sure we shouldn't go through that wood, it does look wild.

TOM: *(Pulls away)* Something is pulling me that way, I can't help it Lucy — I can't help it Lucy — I can't help it...
(NIGHTSHADE beckons TOM)
I'm coming, I'm coming, wait for me.

LUCY: Tom, Tom, don't leave me, don't leave me.

(She runs after him. NIGHTSHADE leads TOM in and out of 'trees' confusing him. LUCY follows)

GARDENIA: *(Enters right. To audience)*
I cannot find that naughty pair
Have you seen them, are they here?
Inside the wood, oh surely not
My words of warning they've forgot
I'll look and maybe help them out
If you should see them, give a shout
Say Tom and Lucy loud and clear
Then I shall know when they are near.

(FAIRY GARDENIA enters wood to find Tom and Lucy — business with two fairies, Tom, Lucy and Trees)

LUCY: *(Sitting down)* It's no good, I'm too tired to go any further — I shall have to stay here. I wish we'd done as the Old Woman said —

she told us not to come through this wood — I am frightened. *(Begins to cry)*

GARDENIA: *(Wearing cloak over fairy costume)*
Lucy do not sit and cry
Come with me, first wipe your eye
I'll make the path for you quite clear
Although you don't deserve it, dear
Then soon you'll be at journey's end
To find your professorial friend.

LUCY: *(Downstage)* I don't know who you are but I shall be glad to have your help, thank you. Tom, Tom, where are you — I'm going to be shown the way out of this dreadful wood.

TOM: Oh, Lucy, I am pleased to see you — I thought I'd lost you — it's all my fault — *I* said we should come through the wood, I should have listened to you.

LUCY: Never mind Tom, a kind lady is going to show us the way. Oh she's gone but I think I can hear her calling, come along, quickly. *(GARDENIA gently calls leading them out of the wood. Trees bend gracefully down when touched by GARDENIA'S wand making the way clear)*

LUCY: Tom, Tom we're safe — look there is the place we're looking for — hurry we're nearly there.

[Runs back to TOM then exits right

TOM: I'm coming Lucy.

[Exits right

NIGHTSHADE: *(Appears from trees)*
I've looked and looked amongst the trees
Where have they gone. do tell me please?
It's that Gardenia. that I'll bet
But never mind I'll beat her yet.

[Exit left)

GARDENIA: *(To audience)*
She's not very nice, don't you agree?
I'd not invite her round for tea
But I'll try to beat her at her game
Then I'll add F.C.S. after my name.

[Exit)

CURTAIN

END OF SCENE I

Scene 2

In front of Curtains.

WIDOW: *(Enters left. Talking to herself)* I wish Tom would come back soon — if only the magic tractor had not been broken, the work would have been done and the Baron could not have taken my land.

(BILL and BEN enter right)

BILL: Hullo, Missus.

WIDOW: Hullo, Ben.

BILL: No, I'm Bill — Ben's the other one.

BEN: Hullo, Missus.

WIDOW: Hullo, other one.

BEN: I'm Ben.

WIDOW: Well, if you're Bill and you're Ben, I'd better be 'little weed' *(Imitation of Flower Pot Men and Weed)* Do any of you children remember them? No, how about Mum and Dad then — you're old enough. I don't really have anything to joke about. I'm not very happy.

BEN: We'll cheer you up — we're rather good at spreading things aren't we, Bill.

BILL: It's usually muck, Ben.

BEN: Er yes, Bill but I was thinking more of happiness.

(Either sing song or:-)

BILL: *(To Audience)* You thought we were going to sing a song there.

BEN: So did the producer.

BILL and BEN: *(Together)* But we forgot the words!

[Exit

BARON: *(Enters)* Oh, ho, and who have we here? The poor Widow Lackpenny!

WIDOW: *(Falsely jovial)* How do you do, Your Worship, Your Grace...er...

BARON: *(Sternly)* And what are you doing about your fields, I see only one field has been ploughed. You know I shall reclaim the farm unless it is finished by next Tuesday.

WIDOW: Oh it will be Baron, I promise you.

BARON: Why not give it up my good woman, it is too much for you to manage.

WIDOW: I will not give it up — I can look after the farm just as well as you.

BARON: Rubbish, of course you can't. Why I can do anything better than you.

WIDOW: Oh no you can't.

BARON: *(Very cross)* Oh yes I can.

SONG - Anything You Can Do.

BARON: You're an impossible woman. I'll have that land you'll see.
[Exeunt

END OF SCENE 1

Scene 2

(Curtain up on Professor's Factory)

TOM: *(Entering backwards)* This looks like the place, Lucy.

LUCY: What's that Tom? It looks like a dragon.

TOM: It *is* a dragon!

LUCY: He likes sweets, remember what the old woman said?

TOM: But which sweets?

(DRAGON roars and lashes tail.)

LUCY: *(Approaching dragon very carefully)* Hullo Dragon, how are you today? I think I have something for you in my pocket.

(DRAGON roars)

TOM: He doesn't sound very good tempered.

LUCY: If he eats a lot of sweets, he's probably got toothache. *(To audience)* Is there a dentist in the house? *(To audience)* Now which sweets do you think he'd like? If we find the right ones, he might let us pass. Liquorice Allsorts? No. Peppermint creams? No. *(Continue list)* Lollipops? *(DRAGON reacts favourably to this)* Yes.

(DRAGON enjoys lollipops and TOM and LUCY go past him to meet the PROFESSOR)

TOM: Professor?

PROFESSOR: What.

TOM: I was addressing you politely, Professor.

PROFESSOR: I know. What.

TOM: Well, I shall tell you *what* after we are introduced. This is Lucy and I am Tom.

PROFESSOR: And I am professor...What?

TOM: I wish you wouldn't keep saying 'what' I was taught that it isn't very polite.

PROFESSOR: You silly young man, that is my name — you've heard of Doctor Who I presume — a friend of mine by the way — often pops in by Tardis, lands in *(Local)* Airport, well I am Professor What.

LUCY: We're very sorry Professor, we'd *forgotten* your name.

PROFESSOR: *(Very bustly all the time)* That's all right, that's all right. Now then, now then. What is it, what do you want, I'm very busy.

TOM: We hope you may be able to help us.

PROFESSOR: Yes, yes, yes, but how?

TOM: We are very poor you see and cannot afford to buy a tractor.

PROFESSOR: I understand that, my boy, but what do you want me to do?

TOM: A kind fairy — it must have been a fairy — gave us a magic tractor called Tinny, but now poor Tinny will not go.

PROFESSOR: Why not?

LUCY: I think someone has stolen the thingumajig.

PROFESSOR: The thingumajig?

TOM: Well, it used to stick out of the top — now it is not there and I cannot find it anywhere.

LUCY: We cannot buy a magic thingumajig anywhere even at *(local shop)*.

PROFESSOR: Thingumajigs are very difficult to make — you see, you have to have a special woffle, then you twist it in a marleypooh, after that it takes a great deal of misky masking and a pull of twenty megametres — hmmmmmm *very difficult. (He makes actions to suit)*

LUCY: Oh dear, what are we going to do?

TOM: If the fields are not tended properly, the Baron who lives next door will take our land and my mother and I will be turned out.

LUCY: *(Beginning to cry)* And I shall never see Tom again.

PROFESSOR: Now, now, I said *difficult* to make — I did not say *impossible*. This is my workshop — I will see what I can do.

(LUCY and TOM look round and see the Assembly line — girls all in black with silver foil hands and hats, linked with blue piping)

PROFESSOR: Here is my assembly line — just a few adjustments and hey presto. I'll switch on.
(Assembly line goes into action — Professor switches on by lifting an arm, screws an ear etc. He collects the finished article at the end of line and switches off machine)
This I believe, is what you are seeking.

LUCY: Tom, is...is that a thingumajig?

TOM: Yes, Lucy — that is a thingumajig.

LUCY: Oh, Professor... *(Giving him a kiss)* ...you are clever.)

PROFESSOR: I know my dear, I know.

TOM: *(Delighted)* Thank you — now I can make Tinny go again, the farm will be safe.

LUCY: Let us hurry back and tell your mother. Goodbye, Professor and thank you. *(Excited she waves to PROFESSOR and waits for TOM at side of stage)*

TOM: Thank you, Professor — I haven't any money, how can I pay you?

PROFESSOR: Get along with you — I don't need money. Go now, be happy.

LUCY and TOM: Goodbye, goodbye.

[Exit left PROFESSOR fusses about. Enter DEADLY NIGHTSHADE somewhat breathless. To audience)

NIGHTSHADE: I've lost them, now where did they go?
Tell me quickly, don't be slow
If you don't tell me double quick
I'll cast a spell and make you sick.

(She asks audience which way — goes off opposite way to TOM and LUCY)

CURTAIN

(Traditional song that audience can join in, and involving children (up on stage) In front of Curtain. WIDOW LACKPENNY helped by BILL and BEN)

END OF SCENE 2

Scene 3

Front of Curtains — other FAIRIES and PIXIE on stage when TEACHER comes in.

TEACHER: The time has come to fail or pass
The fairies you saw in my class
And if they have been doing good
As we know fairies always should
A good report they'll get from me
And a certificate you will see
Come, Bluebell, you'll be the first to tell
How you used your magic spell.

BLUEBELL: I helped a boy across the road
He quite forgot his Green Cross Code
I stopped a bus, it was coming fast
And made it wait till the boy had passed.

(TEACHER FAIRY nods wisely and gives certificate)

TEACHER: Next Fairy please, ah Poppy dear
Your turn to tell, come, have no fear

POPPY: I saw a little pussycat stuck up a great big tree
It's whiskers were a-quivering, it was so sad to see
I used my spell to make a wind, the branches then were bending
So little puss could scramble down, it was a happy ending.

(POPPY collects her certificate)

TEACHER: Buttercup, Buttercup, come and tell
If like the others, you've done well.

BUTTERCUP: Mortals have pensions when they age
The man at the Post Office stamps each page
But Mrs Smith had lost her book
And didn't know where else to look
So she cried and cried and was upset
And would, I think, have been crying yet
But I whispered in her ear and said
She'd find it under the spare room bed.

(Collects certificate)

TEACHER: Rose it is your turn, now to confess
If it was failure or success.

ROSE: Teacher I have been a dunce
My good deeds failed more times than once
Back to school I must return
My fairy law again to learn. *(Cries)*

PIXIE: *(Forward)*
Oh Fairy Rose, please don't cry
Have this *(Pause and produce leaf)* leaf to wipe your eye
I love you Rose, so let us marry *(Kneel)*
For you I'll gladly fetch and carry.

ROSE: Yes please dear Pixie — let's be one
And with this learning I'll be done. *(Embrace)*

TEACHER: Lobelia, come and stand just here
We want to know what you did dear.

LOBELIA: I could not think just what to do to earn my F.C.S.
I knew that I was meant to use my spell for happiness
I found some little orphan boys who had no Mums or Dads
No one to buy them bicycles like other little lads
I magicked up an Uncle, a rich old man was he
He gave both boys a bicycle and took them home to tea.

TEACHER: Godetia now, it is you
To tell me dear what you did do.

GODETIA: The snow was falling thick and fast
As busy shoppers hurried past
The old man stood in ragged dress
No one noticed his distress
I saw that he was frail and cold
No one to care that he was old
So to the hearts of a rich pair
With more than enough for them to share
Brought, with my spell the happy thought
To share with him the gifts they'd bought.

(Collects certificate)

TEACHER: Gardenia dear, did you do well?
I hope you did not waste your spell.

GARDENIA: Let me tell you what I've done
For an old woman and her son
She was poor...her fields unploughed
No time or help for her allowed

By next door wealthy land tycoon
Who was to take her farm quite soon
I stopped all that with Tinny Tractor
Now she can afford to buy Max Factor.

TEACHER: You have done well as I knew you would
For you are sweet and kind and good. *(Gives Certificate)*
Now Deadly Nightshade, I think it's your turn
What have you done your diploma to earn?

NIGHTSHADE: What soppy silly fairies these
(To Audience)
All trying oh so hard to please
Well I've done no good or kindly deed
So your old certificate I'll not need.

TEACHER: In fairyland you cannot stay
Go at once, go right away
Go to the rear end of the hall *(Points to rear of hall)*
We do not want you here at all.

(NIGHTSHADE goes to back through audience)

GARDENIA: Oh, Teacher, can't we make her change
There must be something we can arrange
If all the children we see before us
Wish very hard and say in chorus
'Deadly Nighshade, please be good'
It might just work...do you think it could?
Come children, close your eyes quite tight
And wish with all your main and might.

TEACHER: We will try then, let us see
What will happen, One, Two, Three.

(FAIRIES lead from front of stage to audience)
'Deadly Nightshade, please be good'

(NIGHTSHADE comes from back of hall, looking different — change of cloak, lights etc)

NIGHTSHADE: I feel so strange, all light and airy
Ever so good, not at all contrary
(Comes up centre aisle. To audience on either side)
How wonderful to see you all
Filling the seats in the *(Local)* Hall.

GARDENIA: Your wishing worked, I said it would
You *can* change bad things into good.

(The two FAIRIES kiss on both cheeks and others cluster round making fuss of bad fairy)

TEACHER: *(To audience)*
Shall I give her this, like her friends in class
And let her have a...grade six pass?

(Curtain down on NIGHTSHADE receiving certificate)

END OF SCENE 3

Scene 4

Back at the farm

WIDOW: Isn't it wonderful — Tom has returned with another thingumajig and now Tinny Tractor will go again. The fields are neat and tidy and that wicked old Baron Grabalott won't be able to tell the land tribunal that I am a bad tenant.

BARON: *(From right)* Come, Bill and Ben — look at the way this old woman neglects the land — we shall have something to tell the tribunal next week and then all this will be mine ha-ha!

(BEN goes to side of stage and looks off)

BEN: *(Rubbing hands together)* But, Baron, the land isn't neglected — the ploughing is done — come and look.

BARON: *(Looks where BEN is pointing off stage)*
Ha! How has she done this? Now I shall not be able to claim it back.

BILL: I know how you *could* get the land, master. *(Whispers in ear of BARON)*

BARON: Capital, capital, ho, ho, ho. It might not be such a bad idea, I'm lonely. *(Advances towards WIDOW)* Good day to you my good woman, I see the farm work is all up to date. I was going to offer to lend you these two fellows here to help you but you will not need them now.

WIDOW: *(To audience)* This is a change — I'll string him along. Oh Baron, you are too, too kind but I think all will be well now.

BARON: Well, you know if there is anything, just anything I can do to help, you only have to ask — it is time we became more... *(Sidling up to her)* ...neighbourly.

WIDOW: How can I trust you? Five minutes ago you were all set to throw me off the farm.

BARON: *Trust me?* Trust me? Of course you can trust me. There isn't a more trustworthy man in the land.

WIDOW: *(To audience)* Should I trust him? No, I don't trust you and I wish you would go away.

BARON: Very well, but first let me tell you a little story, then you must decide.
Music from 'Tit Willow' from the Mikado.
At the gate of her farmhouse the poor widow sang

'No husband, no husband, no husband'
The Baron he'd said to her 'Why do you stand
Singing husband, no husband, no husband?'
'Is it lack of a husband, oh widow' he cried
'And a longing for masculine help by your side?'
With a nod of her poor little head she replied
'I've no husband, no husband, no husband'
He slapped at his chest as he watched her stand there
That widow, dear widow, dear widow
And the thought came to him that she might come to care
That widow, dear widow, dear widow
She sobbed and she sighed and a hiccup she gave
'My husband lies deep in the earth in his grave
From this loneliness Sire, won't somebody save
This widow, this widow, this widow?'
Now I feel just as sure as my name's Grabalott
Dear widow, dear widow, dear widow
That together we'd tie a true loving knot
Dear widow, dear widow, dear widow
But if you remain in your solitary state
Like that Baron I'll pine for the want of a mate
As I breathe my last breath you will hear my sad cry
Oh widow, dear widow, dear widow.

WIDOW: *(Sobbing)* Oh Baron. *(Wrings out hanky.*

(During song there must be comic reactions from BILL and BEN but must not detract from story in song)

BARON: Well you know if there is anything, just...
(Enter TOM and LUCY)

LUCY: Hullo Father, I didn't know you were here.

BARON: Er, I'm just visiting the Widow here.

TOM: Does this mean we can be friends too — if so...

BARON: It seems to me that if the two farms were run as a co-operative...

BEN: *(Aside to audience)* Crafty old so-and-so!

WIDOW: I'll co-operate with you any time Baron. *(To audience)* Well, he is rather handsome and I haven't anyone to warm my feet on these cold nights.

TOM: Do I take it Sire, that you will have no objection if I ask your daughter to marry me.

BARON: Is that what you want, Lucy?

LUCY: Oh yes please, Father.
BARON: Then it shall be so.
LUCY: *(Kissing Father)* Thank you dear Father — I'm so happy.

SONG— Music from TRIO H.M.S.Pinafore

LUCY:
Never mind the why and wherefore
Love can level ranks and therefore
Though the Baron's station's mighty
Though stupendous be his brain
Though her tastes are mean and flighty
And his fortune poor and plain.

(CHORUS — BARON, LUCY and TOM)
Ring the merry bells with joy
And rend the air with warbling wild
For the union of a poor boy
With a noble Baron's child.

BARON: For a noble Baron's daughter.
LUCY: For a gallant Baron's daughter
BARON: And a boy who owns a tractor.
LUCY: That dear boy who owns a tractor.

LUCY and BARON:
Let the air with joy be laden
Rend with songs the air above
For the union of a maiden
With the boy who owns her love.

BARON:
Never mind the why and wherefore
Love can level ranks and therefore
Though your agricultural station
In my set could scarcely pass
Though you occupy a station
In the lower middle class.

(CHORUS — BARON, LUCY and TOM)
Ring the merry bells with joy
And rend the air with warbling wild
For the union of a poor boy
With a noble Baron's child.

BARON: For a noble Barons daughter.
LUCY: For a gallant Baron's daughter.
BARON: And a boy who owns a tractor.
LUCY: That dear boy who owns a tractor.

LUCY AND BARON: Let the air with joy be laden
Ring the merry bells with joy
For the union of a maiden
For her union with her boy
Rend with songs the air above
For the boy who owns her love
Rend with songs the air above
For the boy who owns her love.

(During the chorus BILL and BEN execute comic dance entering either side from wings and crossing behind singers upstage. This must only be done during chorus or it will detract from song. At end of song all dance off in comic fashion)

TINNY TRACTOR: So each one here has found a friend
The way that pantomime should end
But no one loves poor Tinny T
Is there nobody meant for me?
But what is this far down the aisle *(Seen at back of hall)*
Approaching with beguiling smile
It's little Urn, but not the mister
With hairy legs, this one's his sister
Do you think that she has come to say
With me upon the farm she'll stay.

(URNITRUDE must make entrance through centre of audience if possible while TINNY speaks)

URNITRUDE: My pure white heart with fondness true
Is brimming over with love for you
For long I've loved you, Tinny dear
But you never noticed I was here
Oh Tinny, make this my happiest day
Let's travel together life's milky way.

TINNY TRACTOR: Oh, Urnitrude please do me mine
We'll stand together rain or shine.

(Appearance of performers with final song)

CURTAIN

LIGHTING PLOT

Lighting may be simple or sophisticated, depending on facilities available.

ACT I

Scene 1

Cue 1	Page 7	As Curtain rises - Full lighting
Cue 2	Page 10	Enter PIXIE GARY - Fade lighting - spot on PIXIE
Cue 3	Page 10	"...there'll be a spot of bother..." - Full lighting
Cue 4	Page 11	As TOM and WIDOW nod off - Fade lighting - spot GARDENIA's entrance.
Cue 5	Page 12	Enter NIGHTSHADE - sinister lighting or spot.
Cue 6	Page 13	Enter TINNY TRACTOR - full lighting

Scene 2

Cue 7	Page 14	Front Cloth - full lighting
Cue 8	Page 14	Open curtains - full stage lighting
Cue 9	Page 17	LUCY "...on an island where the sun is always shining" Fade to pink lighting.
Cue 10	Page 18	Enter BARON - full lighting

Scene 3

Cue 11	Page 21	Curtains open - Night time - lights in farmhouse go out.
Cue 12	Page 21	Look in the engine - bring lights up or spot tractor
Cue 13	Page 22	Light on in upstairs window
Cue 14	Page 23	Half curtains - bright, full lighting - morning
Cue 15	Page 25	LUCY "...I shall never see you again..." Dim lights as OLD WOMAN enters
Cue 16	Page 26	SONG 'Tomorrow' - gradually bring up full lighting

ACT II

Scene 1

Cue 17	Page 27	Curtains open on Wild Wood - sinister, shadowy light When trees bend gracefully change to warm lighting

Scene 2

Cue 18	Page 30	Front cloth - full lighting
Cue 19	Page 31	Professor's factory - full lighting
Cue 20	Page 33	Assembly line in shadow until switched on, then lit
Cue 21	Page 34	Lower lighting for entry of NIGHTSHADE

Scene 3

Cue 22 Page 35	Front cloth - full lighting
Cue 23 Page 37	When NIGHTSHADE goes to back of hall accompany her change with appropriate lighting effect to enhance transformation from bad to good nature

Scene 4

Cue 24 Page 39	Full lighting
Cue 25 Page 42	TINNY "...so each one..." - dim lighting
Cue 26 Page 42	Enter URNITRUDE - spot then full lighting or large spot on URNITRUDE and TINNY when both on stage together
Cue 27 Page 42	Finalé - Full lighting

SCENERY AND PROPERTIES LIST

ACT I

Scene 1
ON STAGE - Sign pointing to Castle
End of Widow's Farmhouse with broken fence.
Old wooden plough.
Tree with trimmed blackboard hanging from it.
Toadstools.
Large log.
Flower balls, flower skipping rope.

PERSONAL - Mirror, comb (POPPY)
Tinsel trimmed pointer, Book of Fairy Law (TEACHER)
Chalk (NIGHTSHADE)

Scene 2
ON STAGE - Log

Scene 3
ON STAGE - Farmhouse as Sc 1
Metal bucket (to kick)
Ladder
Boxes
Thingumajig (to steal from tractor)

ACT II

Scene 2
ON STAGE - Sweets for dragon
Beer cans
Scientific paraphernalia for Professor's workshop
Flexible piping to link assembly line (girls)
New thingumajig

Scene 3
Certificates for fairies (appropriately decorated)
Large leaf (PIXIE to give ROSE)

Scene 4
'Smart' fence replacing broken one.